做一个好公民

Social Emotional and Multicultural Learning |
Non-Fiction Series

Copyright © 2022 by Level Learning, INC. and Washington Yu Ying PCS™
Original and Edited Text Copyright © 2022 by Washington Yu Ying PCS™

All rights reserved. No part of this book in whole or part may be reproduced without written permission from the publisher.

Published by Level Learning, INC.
Content Contributors:
Washington Yu Ying PCS™
Level Learning - Ya-Ching Chang

Illustrations by: Josh Taira

Leveling classification based on Level Learning standard.
For full description, visit www.levellearning.com

ISBN 978-1-64040-089-4
Simplified Chinese Edition

About Level Learning:
Level Learning provides a literacy focused curriculum specifically designed for K-12 Chinese as a Second Language classrooms. Our program offers 20 levels of specific and detailed objectives, leveled texts and passages, mastery-based online assessment, and analytics to enable data-driven instruction. Level Learning reading curriculum for both literature and informational text emphasize grammar and comprehension skills to help teachers develop confident and independent Chinese language readers. The non-fiction series of books are specifically designed to support our informational text course based on multiple national standards. To learn more about our entire offering, visit www.levellearning.com.

About Washington Yu Ying PCS™:
Washington Yu Ying PCS is a Mandarin English dual language immersion International Baccalaureate (IB) World school. Yu Ying's mission is to inspire and prepare young people to create a better world by challenging them to reach their full potential in a nurturing Chinese/English educational environment. Yu Ying's comprehensive IB, dual immersion curriculum equips students with global competencies for success in the real world. As a leader in immersion education, Yu Ying is determined to advance Chinese language programs and global citizenry education by helping other schools create and strengthen their Chinese programs. For more information, email: products@washingtonyuying.org

每个人都是社会的一部分，让我们生活的社会变得更美好，是每一个公民应尽的责任。所以我们来到学校，除了学习知识以外，还要学习如何做一个好公民。

好公民需要具备五种最重要的品德：诚实、尊重、责任、同情和勇敢。

诚实：诚实是成为好公民最基本的品德。我们要诚实真诚地对待身边的每一个人；诚实地面对自己的错误，不说谎；鼓励身边的每一个人都做诚实守法的好公民。

7

尊重：我们不仅要尊重身边的人，也要尊重我们生活的环境。比如，对人有礼貌，排队守秩序，不大声喧哗，这些是对人的尊重；不乱丢垃圾，做好资源回收，保护自然生态，这些是对环境的尊重。

责任：每个公民都有应尽的责任。对于学生来说，努力读书，对自己的学习负责，就是一个好公民应尽的责任。而成年公民的责任包括：纳税、投票、支持国家建设等。

同情：一个好公民要有同情心，关心和帮助有需要的人。很多人都会尽自己的力量去帮助别人，比如做社区服务或当义工，还可以捐钱给有需要的人。一个好公民应该懂得和别人分享，让更多人生活得更好。

勇气：勇敢地面对不公平，**维护正义**是一种勇气。比如说，看到**性别歧视**或**种族**歧视，一个好公民会勇敢地指出这些不公平。遇到**违法**的行为，也要勇敢地说出来。这样，社会上才会减少歧视和**犯罪**。

成为一个好公民，我们可以让社会变得更美好、更公平，也更安全。除了书中的这些例子，想一想，还有哪些是好公民应尽的责任呢？

Glossary

	Pinyin	English Definition
社会	shè huì	society
部分	bù fèn	part
美好	měi hǎo	beautiful, good
公民	gōng mín	citizen
应	yīng	should
尽	jìn	to the great extent
责任	zé rèn	responsibility
知识	zhī shi	knowledge
如何	rú hé	how
需要	xū yào	need
具备	jù bèi	to have
品德	pǐn dé	character
诚实	chéng shí	to be honest
尊重	zūn zhòng	to respect
责任	zé rèn	to be responsible

	Pinyin	English Definition
同情	tóng qíng	to sympathize
勇敢	yǒng gǎn	brave
基本	jī běn	basic
面对	miàn duì	to face
错误	cuò wù	mistake
说谎	shuō huǎng	to lie
鼓励	gǔ lì	to encourage
守法	shǒu fǎ	to follow the law
环境	huán jìng	surroundings
礼貌	lǐ mào	courtesy, manners
排队	pái duì	to line up
守	shǒu	to observe
秩序	zhì xù	order
喧哗	xuān huá	to make noise or a scene
乱丢	luàn diū	to leave things lying around

Glossary

	Pinyin	English Definition
垃圾	lā jī	garbage
资源	zī yuán	resources
回收	huí shōu	to recycle
保护	bǎo hù	to protect
自然生态	zì rán shēng tài	natural ecosystems
努力	nǔ lì	great effort
负责	fù zé	be responsible
纳税	nà shuì	to pay tax
投票	tóu piào	to vote
支持	zhī chí	to support
建设	jiàn shè	to build
力量	lì liàng	power
社区服务	shè qū fú wù	community service
当	dāng	to be, to do
义工	yì gōng	volunteer

	Pinyin	English Definition
捐钱	juān qián	to donate money
分享	fēn xiǎng	to share
维护	wéi hù	to maintain
正义	zhèng yì	justice
性别	xìng bié	gender
歧视	qí shì	discrimination
种族	zhǒng zú	race
违法	wéi fǎ	to break the law
犯罪	fàn zuì	crime

www.ingramcontent.com/pod-product-compliance
Lightning Source LLC
Chambersburg PA
CBHW041222070526
44584CB00001B/50